The Mind
and
Self-Reflection

A New Way
to
Read with Your Mind

Ron W. Rathbun

QUIESCENCE PUBLISHING
OCEANSIDE, CALIFORNIA

THE MIND AND SELF-REFLECTION
A New Way to Read with Your Mind

This book is an original publication of Quiescence Publishing

PRINTING HISTORY
Quiescence Publishing first edition / January 2010

For information address:
Quiescence Publishing
Post Office Box 373
Oceanside, CA 92049-0373

www.thekelee.org

ISBN: 0-9643519-5-1

PRINTED IN THE UNITED STATES OF AMERICA

Acknowledgements

There are many people I would like to thank...

My mentor Gene, who introduced me to the mind and the beauty that a love of learning can bring into your life.

Nikki Feldman, for being the dedicated worker bee that she is. She knows that her efforts are going to impact the long-term future of this planet.

Jo Phillips, for her diligent copy editing and caring nature. The world needs more fairy princesses.

Lavana, she has been by my side from the beginning. She knows that the best is yet to come.

There are many others to thank and they know who they are, however, their story will be told at a later date.

*When self-reflection is part
of your life,
self-understanding is sure to follow.
How do you define your thoughts
and
what do you do with them
in your life?*

—Ron W. Rathbun

Contents

Introduction

Most of what is taught in the world is to study what others have done with their thoughts, which is well and good; however, what about your thoughts?

All great discoveries are made when someone thinks outside the brain. Thinking outside the brain is in actuality when someone perceives with the mind. To study your mind, you must learn how to read it first. If you want to understand why you think what you do, you must learn how to read your thoughts, with your mind.

To understand your mind, you must understand how your conscious awareness operates. Your conscious awareness is who is reading these words right now. It is a term that describes how consciously aware you are in each given moment. Your conscious awareness can work in either brain function associated with thinking and analyzation, or it can work in mind function associated with mentally feeling.

At any given moment, our conscious awareness can either think or mentally feel. We all know what thinking is, most of the time it seems hard to stop the chatter in one's head. If you are distracted by chatter, it is hard to learn anything. Have you ever read something and not understood what you read? This is the brain reading, but not understanding.

If you want to understand what you read, you must learn to access the mind first and allow the brain to memorize second. One way to spot the difference between brain and mind is the brain uses a hard form of analytical energy whereas the mind uses a soft subtle form of energy. The brain uses a lot of energy; the mind uses an effortless energy.

This is a diagram of an ancient phenomenon called the Kelee® (pronounced "key-lee"). I am showing you this diagram because I want you to try to read the quotes in this book with your mind, instead of your brain. The easiest way to get out of the brain and into the mind is to feel your conscious awareness where your heart is located. Ironically enough, all you have to do is feel where you love from and you will be in mind. It is from your mind that you can begin to love learning.

Everyone at one time or another has felt emotion well up from within. If you can read this book from where your heart is, you will begin to enter into a deeper level of mind and understanding.

This is where both hemispheres of your brain are ⟶

The line at eye level is called the surface of the mind ⟶ (The surface of the mind is where your thoughts are right now.)

Now, feel your conscious awareness where you feel your heart ⟶

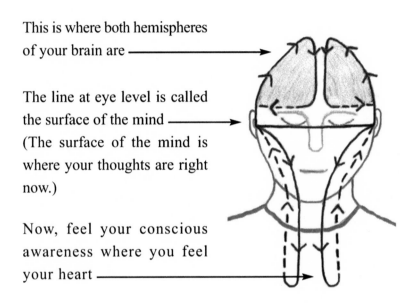

    This book offers a new way to learn. If you practice this new way of understanding your mind, it will change the way you learn about your life and how you feel about yourself in a profoundly beautiful way.

*Do you feel your life
with
your heart?*

Thinking is here ⎯⎯⎯⎯⎯⎯⎯→

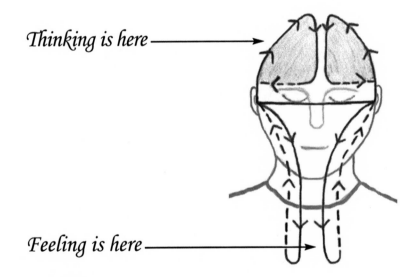

Feeling is here ⎯⎯⎯⎯⎯⎯⎯⎯→

When you start helping yourself,
you
start the process of becoming
your own inspiration.
How inspiring are you
with yourself?
If not, why not?

The day only means something,

if

it means something

to you.

What do your days mean to you?

*A warm smile
is an acknowledgement
of what is right.
How often do you smile
and
for what reason?*

*T*here's nothing
by nature
inherently wrong with us,
we create or accept it!
Why create or accept
that
which hurts you
when you have a choice?

*W*hen you
can get out of your own way,
it's easier to get things done.
Do you get in your own way
and why?

*If you give yourself
half a chance,
you'll have one!
Are you hard on yourself,
and
does it help?*

*Your life
is not what's upcoming,
it's how you feel
in your shoes right now.
Do you feel the steps you take?*

If you are to find your way,

it must be by your steps,

not somebody else's.

After all,

who can move your feet for you?

You can't be left behind,

when

you know how to walk yourself.

Why don't you walk

the way

you want to walk?

If you know balance,

you

are not thrown

off-balance.

Are you thrown off-balance

by your own thoughts?

*It's not wise
to be so driven in life
that you drive mindlessly.
Do you ever do things
and
wonder why you did them?*

*W*hen production
is more important
than people,
people produce less.
*D*o people like the way
you treat them?

*Patience is something
worth waiting for
when
you realize
what the alternative is.
Where has impatience ever taken you?*

*It's amazing
that anyone
would fight with their life,
so as
to not enjoy it.
Have you ever done this
and why?*

*You're never too busy
to enjoy yourself
when
you like what you do.
How often
do you
enjoy yourself?*

*L*ife
has a wonderful taste to it
when you are
involved in its splendor.
Do you enjoy good taste
in your life?

Only when you have good taste

in your soul

will you have great taste

in your life.

How do you

develop good taste in your life?

The purest part of doing
comes from
the purest part of being.
How do you find
your being?

Chapter Two

Learning

Do you care
if
you are learning?

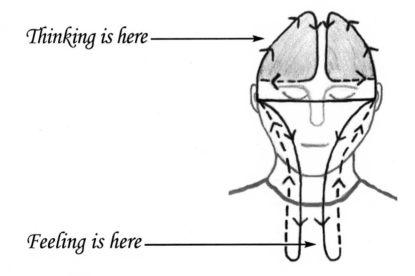

Thinking is here ——————→

Feeling is here ——————→

Life
primarily is not about
what you teach others,
it's about
what you learn yourself.
How well have you learned?

Your mind

is open to every answer

if you

allow them to come!

Do you know

how to open your mind?

All life experiences
mean something,
when you're open to them.
Do you hold back
from opening to what life has to offer
and why?

*There is only one way
to start learning:
when you're ready.
Why would you not be ready
to learn?*

Until
you're ready to accept,
you do not.
What do you allow into your mind
and
is it good?

You cannot answer a question

for someone

who does not want

to hear the truth.

Do you want to hear the truth,

even when

it proves you incorrect?

A teacher's responsibility

is to teach,

however,

it is a student's responsibility

to learn.

Do you understand how you learn?

Discipline
does not have to be hard,
in point of fact
it's beautiful,
it leads us to learning.
Do you like to learn?
If not, why not?

*Most of what
we are looking for
is what we don't understand,
because
that is where we need to learn.
What do you know
about
your learning process?*

Everything
you have a problem with
shows you
your weakness.
What do you know about
your weaknesses,
and what do they teach you?

*Misunderstanding
is not a fault,
it is only the process of learning.
Do you know
what you misunderstand?*

Even when things go wrong,

there is no fault,

only learning.

Do you learn

from your mistakes?

It is ignorance
to blame people
for what they don't know;
our learning process is never a fault!
Do you blame others
for their lack of experience
and what
they do not know?

The harder the experience,

the more valuable the lesson.

Have you ever forgotten a hard lesson?

More importantly,

did it

need to be learned that way?

Hardship is strength

being earned.

Take this to heart

and

you will succeed.

Are you successful

with what you're learning?

It is not wise to walk in the dark

without a light.

Does your mind's light of awareness

free you from fear

and

illumine your way?

Good luck is seeing
with awareness,
bad luck is seeing
without it.
Do you
have more good luck
or bad?

*Thoughts that are meaningful
are thoughts
you have learned to value.
Do you have meaningful thoughts
in your life,
and
where do they originate?*

*How do you feel
about
how you spend time?*

Thinking is here

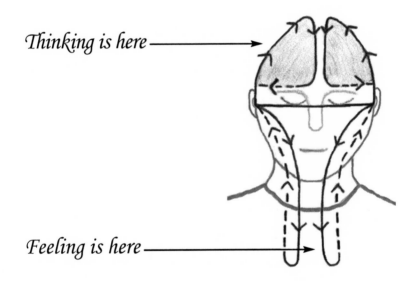

Feeling is here

*Life experience
is much richer when you are not
thinking about time.
What determines the richness of your time?*

Quality time is measured
first and foremost
by how you feel in your day.
How do you feel
at the end of your day,
fulfilled or disappointed
and
who decides that?

You really cannot lose time,

unless

you are not paying attention!

How often are you distracted?

And the biggest question,

why and by what?

You only need to deal with

what the day brings,

nothing more.

Is not

today's work

enough for one day?

*You cannot sail
with the winds of tomorrow,
today!
If you are thinking about tomorrow,
are you living today?*

The farther away
you see things,
the less they mean
right now.
Can you be in the now
and
the future at the same time?

Patience is an understanding

that

timing is everything.

Do you have good timing

or

bad timing?

When you don't need patience

is always

when you have it.

Do you know how to patiently wait?

If not, why?

Patience used in the right way,
is called enjoying yourself
in the moment.
Do you enjoy yourself?

Being on a strict time schedule,

on personal time,

is not fun!

Do you like your off time?

If not, why?

Give yourself
more personal time,
and you will have more of it!
If you don't give yourself time,
who will?

*The only way to be grounded
in your life
is to be present in it.
Can you be grounded in your life
and somewhere else
at the same time?*

*The degree of how well
you feel grounded
is dependent on how well
you feel the ground beneath you.
Are you present in each moment?
If not, why?*

When you open
to the present,
you can let go of the past.
How much of the time
are you in the past
or
in the present?

*H*ow can a hurtful thought
from the past
put you down today?
How do your hurts from the past
affect you,
and how do you free yourself
from them today?

A regret of the past,
is a regret in the present!
How many times has a regret
given you grief,
and why would you ever want
to hold onto something that hurts you?

Our mind can be

a clean slate

if

we can let go of the hurtful past.

Do you know how

to clean your mind?

*You don't have to be perfect
in your life,
just moving in that direction.
Are you hard on yourself
or
helpful with yourself?*

*Are you heartfelt
with
yourself?*

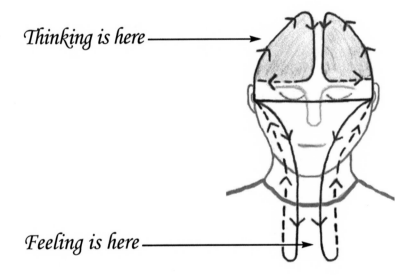

Thinking is here

Feeling is here

*The biggest mystery in the world
is you.
What do you know about yourself?*

If you are looking for a reason to be,
other than to be yourself,
that's what you will find.
Can you be other
than yourself?

To be
your own best friend,
you have got to allow yourself
to be so.
Are you good to yourself?
If not, why?

*You must know
how you feel about yourself
to know how you feel
about the world around you.
How well do you feel
and understand yourself?*

*If you have already determined
who you are,
you forego
your living interaction of change.
Are you living from your past,
or are you growing
in your understanding of you
in the present?*

*Your relationship
with yourself
is not something you make,
it's something you feel.
Do you make your feelings
or experience them?*

The relationship
you have with yourself
is not that different than the relationship
you have with others.
Does not what you share with another
come from you?
What is the quality of what you share?

What your thoughts denote
does not need to be important to others;
it would be wise
if they were important to you.
Are you important to yourself?

*You don't have to be something
to the outside world
to be something to yourself.
Can you feel good about yourself
independent
of the outside world's opinion?*

You cannot be comfortable
with the world
until you are comfortable
with being alone with yourself.
How comfortable are you alone?

*The time you spend alone
with your thoughts
is
where you'll find the purest part
of you.
Would it not be wise
to spend more time there?*

The less you look to others,
the more you find
in yourself.
What have you found
in yourself?

*Your heart's
own beautiful feeling
is its best protection
against what demeans you?
Are you protected
by the beauty of self-understanding?*

Be more concerned
with your inside appearance,
and
you will be less concerned
with your outside appearance.
What determines how good you feel,
how you look outside
or
how you feel inside?

*Finding your self-image
is not something
you find outside yourself,
it's something you find within.
How do you feel about yourself
without a mirror?*

*F*rom the reflection

of

what you don't have,

you will find

what you do have,

yourself.

Have you found yourself?

*You can only lose
what
is not yours!
What is it
that you can really possess
other than yourself?
And can you really lose yourself?*

Being who you are

is

far more beautiful than

being

who you are not.

How can you be other

than you?

*If you don't like the way
you see yourself,
who can change it for you?
There is only one answer,
isn't there?
You!*

*K*now yourself.
The question is,
how do
you do it?
Do you have a way?

Chapter Five

Relationships

*How do you feel
about
your relationships?*

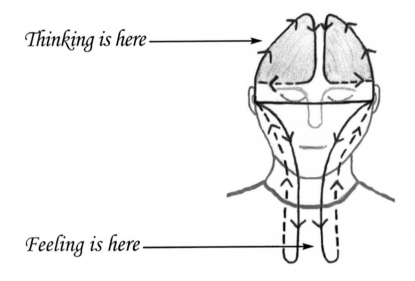

Thinking is here ⎯⎯⎯⎯→

Feeling is here ⎯⎯⎯⎯→

When you change yourself
to be with another,
you lose yourself.
Why would you want to lose yourself
in the presence of another?

A measure
from another person's perspective
is not a measure of you
at all.
Do others ever decide what
you should do,
and why do you allow it?

*There's a difference
between
an influence being imposed upon you
and
you opening up to an influence.
What influences you
in your life?*

*Some people
take you away from who you are,
and some people
bring you closer to who you are.
Who do you
want
to be around you?*

*The easiest way
to not be deceived
is to not be
deceptive with yourself.
Have you ever been dishonest with yourself,
and
did you like it?*

How we help people
is by
being real with them.
If you are not yourself with another,
who are you?

The best thing you can do

for others

is to not take away their responsibility

to care for themselves.

Do you help

or

hinder others with your actions?

Lending an ear
without judgment
will calm a lot of problems.
Can you listen without judgment?

If you make something
an issue,
it will be!
Do you create issues for yourself
or others,
and why?

It is not for you

to excuse another for their actions;

we are all responsible

for our actions!

Are you

responsible for your actions?

*Everyone's responsibility
is to solve their own stupidity,
not another's!
Do you not have enough to solve
about your own life?
Why take time to criticize others?*

*When you learn
to not do for others,
they learn to do for themselves.
Can you allow others
to learn
for themselves?*

When you have learned
to be careful
with your own thoughts,
you will be careful with another's.
Do your thoughts hurt others?

Another person's lack of care
should never
be a reflection of you.
Is it wise to listen
to those
who hold no value of life?

Regardless
of how another person treats you,
it's up to you
whether or not you accept it.
Why accept another's negative view of you?
It's hurtful!

It is not wise

to follow the disharmonious thoughts

of others,

unless disharmony

is where you want to go.

Are you attracted to the dark side of life?

If so, why?

If you like to fight,
you will attract fighting!
Is this wise
and is it
what you want to do?

*W*hen a thought of anger lashes out,
quite often
souls are left bleeding and mentally abused.
You can heal a physical wound,
but how do you
take back your hurtful thought
from another's mind?

Anger, at its best,

is an emotion

for self-protection not retaliation.

Has retaliation ever felt good?

So why do it?

When you
control the experience of life,
you stop experiencing it.
When you have control issues,
do you like yourself?

It is craziness to think

you can control

another human being.

Have you ever tried to do this,

and

is this not mental slavery?

*H*ow other people are

is

how other people are.

What do they

have to do with you?

It is an illusion
that you
have control over another.
Who in the world
have you ever really completely controlled?

Let the world be
and
you will be free from it.
What can you really control
in the world?

If you inspire people with an opportunity
to be great,
then that's what
they will give back to you.
How do you inspire yourself
and others?

Love
in relationships
is the acceptance of each other
and
what life feels like
when it's properly lived.
Do you live properly?
If not, why?

*Do you feel good
about
your thoughts?*

Thinking is here

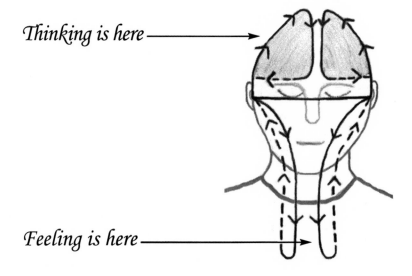

Feeling is here

*Tend the beauty
of your own thoughts,
and you will grow beauty
beyond imagination.
What beauty grows in your mind?*

When you do not value your own thoughts,

self-worth is nowhere

to be found.

Why would you ever

think

your thoughts are worthless?

*You can't be comfortable
with thoughts
that are uncomfortable.
How comfortable are you
with your thoughts?*

It is not wise

to move faster than your thoughts

will allow

or

you may trip over them.

Do you ever find yourself

tripping

over your words

and why?

*The only way
to lose yourself in thought,
is to not
understand your thought process.
What do you learn from your thoughts?*

*Learning from your thoughts
happens
when you spend time
with them.
What can you learn from your thoughts
if you
do not study them?*

The more humble

you are

with your thoughts,

the more open you are to them.

Do you want to be open to your thoughts

and

learn from them?

Don't doubt your thoughts,

study them.

Ask yourself,

"Why do I have

the thoughts I do?"

*Your own self-study
of your thoughts
is ultimately what yields
your deepest rewards in understanding.
How many deep rewards
have you experienced?*

Any thought that touches your mind,
is a relationship with life.
What kind of relationship do you have
with your thoughts?

How is another to decide

for you

the thoughts you should think?

Who can think for you?

No one feels through another's mind,

you feel through your own

or

you do not.

What are your thoughts telling you?

If you do not like how you feel
about your own thoughts,
what are you sharing
with another?
Anything worthwhile?
Do you know
you can change them?

*W*hen you enjoy your mind,

you do not need to be entertained

by another.

Are you pleased with your thoughts

and

are they enjoyable?

Another person cannot save you

from your own thoughts,

however,

you can!

Do you not want to feel good

about yourself?

If not, why?

You cannot cast a shadow

into light.

Do you stand more

in the light of your awareness

or

in the shadow of dark thought?

Where do you

think

you feel more safe?

One must not be afraid
to stand alone
within the infinite
or
you will find
yourself trapped by the finite.
Are you trapped by limiting thoughts?

*If someone is irritating you
and
you can't stand it,
whose problem is it,
theirs or yours?
Are you trapped by thoughts
you don't like
and why?*

Your mind is your own

and

no one else's!

If you think otherwise,

someone else is controlling your life.

Who is in control of your thoughts

and

your life?

You're only imprisoned
by that
which you think controls you.
What really controls you in your life,
and
what of your free will?

*It would be wise
to put energy
into what can be done,
not
what cannot be done.
Do you waste thought energy?*

When thoughts of worry

evolve

to thoughts of concern,

something constructive can be done!

Why have thoughts of worry

if

you can do nothing

about them?

You cannot be responsible

for yourself

if

you are not responsible

for your negative thoughts.

How responsible

are you

with your thoughts?

Often,
it takes letting go
of something bitter
to find
something sweet.
Are your thoughts sweet?

There are many forms of great thought,
the ultimate is your own.
What have you done
of significance
with your thoughts?

Do not underestimate

the power

you have to change yourself

with the right thoughts.

Do you understand your thoughts

and

how they manifest destiny?

*W*hen it comes to asking good questions,

ask yourself this one!

Where do I go from this moment

and

how will my thoughts

affect my decisions ahead?

You don't have to be

somewhere else

to find where you are.

How often are your thoughts

where you are?

_Do you
understand
your emotions?_

Thinking is here —————→

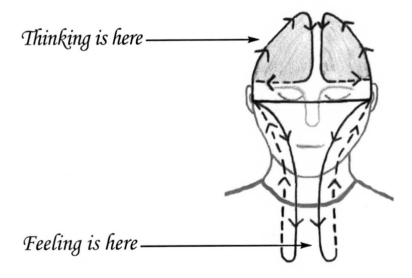

Feeling is here —————→

Beautiful emotion

is its own

validation.

Why would another

need to validate

how good you feel about yourself?

*T*rust is learning
how you feel about yourself,
not
how others feel about you.
Do you trust how you feel?
If not, why?

When you trust what you think

by what you feel,

you see what's what.

Do your thoughts and feelings agree

with each other?

If not, why?

Trusting yourself

means

never having to worry

that you are unloved.

What good reason can you think of

to not

love yourself?

If you cannot trust yourself,

you will always

live in fear!

Do you trust your mind?

If not, why?

*You cannot depend on another
to deal with that
which you must face alone,
your own fear.
How does fear in your mind
affect you?*

*This is the only moment in time
when you
can face your fearful thoughts
and do something
about them.
What are you doing
about them?*

*You cannot be free
and
be connected to fear
at the same time.
Which are you, fearful or free?*

It is thoughts of love
that
teach us to fly;
it is fearful thoughts
that
weight us down.
Where are your thoughts
more often?

*Love
comes to those
who are open to it.
How do you know
if you
are open to yourself?*

You don't have to be held
by someone
to feel love in you.
Can you be alone
and
feel loved?

You are either an example

of love

or you are not.

Are you a loving being?

If not, why?

What you contribute to others

is

what you have found

in yourself.

What have you found

within you

that is worth giving?

Gifts
are only gifts
when they are given freely.
Do you give freely
or
with strings attached?

The most powerful part of giving

is not

what you give,

it's how you feel while giving.

Does what you give

feel better to you

or

the person you're giving to?

A person who gives

is

not the one

who decides who receives.

Are you giving to receive

or

giving out of the pureness of giving?

*When you
learn to accept yourself,
you will not need
the acceptance of others.
Why does anyone need
to accept you?*

*There is no good reason
to feel bad
about you,
unless you want to!
Why would you ever want
to feel bad?*

*When you can cry
without feeling bad,
you can begin to feel good
about
letting go of emotional pain.
Do your tears help you
or
hurt you?*

*C*are
is the doorway
to all good feeling
in the human experience.
For what reason
would you
ever not want to care?

How do you feel
about
being mindful?

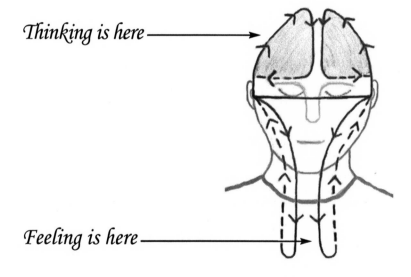

Thinking is here

Feeling is here

When it comes to your mind,

you

are either enhancing it

or

detracting from it.

What are you doing with your mind?

All intelligence starts with

you

paying attention!

If you are not paying attention,

what are you doing?

*Intelligence without wisdom
is trouble.
Is knowledge more important
than how
you
feel about it?*

*K*nowledge
without personal interest
is
knowledge without meaning.
Is what you learn
of
personal interest to you
and does it feel good?

Intelligence
is understanding the world outside you;
wisdom
is understanding the world within you.
Would it be wise
to lead your life
with
intelligence or wisdom?

A wise person learns to read
their life first
and
other people's second.
How well can you read
your life?

*Being mindful
gives you the advantage
of living
from your best qualities,
not your worst.
Which qualities
do you live from most often?*

Mindfulness is the acceptance

that

I am here.

Are you here right now?

The opposite of mindfulness is distraction.
Is something distracting you
from this moment?
If so,
what and why?

If you are not where you are,

you are scattered somewhere else.

Where is that

and

what are you doing there?

The world is not a safe place,

it is only safe,

when you feel safe within.

Do you feel safe in your own mind?

If not, why?

*W*hen you're
in a safe place within,
you will never need to escape yourself.
How can you escape your mind,
and
why would you need to?

Everything feels comfortable

and

in its place

when you feel comfortable

in your space.

How often are you comfortable

in your space?

If you never learn

to say

no thank you,

people never learn

to respect your space!

Do you respect your own space?

*Coming from a good space
inside you
leads to a good place
outside you.
How do you find a good space
in your mind?*

*Never measure your life
when
you're in a bad space!
Take this to heart
and
your life will get easier.
Do you want your life to be
easy or hard?*

It would be wise
to feel
the calmness of mind
not
the roughness of life.
How often are you calm?

If you
have calmed down
a disturbance in your mind,
have you
not effected a good change
in yourself?

*When you
have deep calm
in the mind,
it is difficult to disturb.
How would you
like
to have deep calm
in your mind?*

To find peace,
you must allow yourself
to be peaceful.
How do you find peace in your life
and
how often are you peaceful?

*How do you feel
about
your perceptions of life?*

Thinking is here ——————→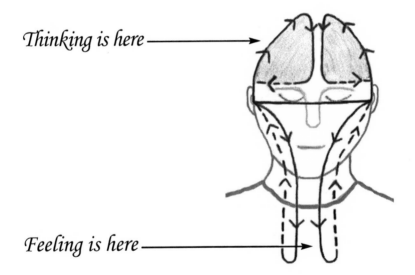

Feeling is here ————————————→

If you want to open your perception,

all you have

to do

is slow down your mind

and see.

Can you see more clearly standing still

or moving?

Life
is only boring
when you cannot perceive it.
Are you bored with your life
and why?

When
life experience enters
your mind,
thought-form images
become the pictures of life.
Do you like what you see before you?

There are many forms of beauty
in the world,
none more beautiful
than
what is before you.
How much beauty do you see?

Beauty
can only be perceived
if
you feel beautiful within.
How often do you feel
your own beauty?

You
determine what you see
by
how you feel within.
Who is controlling
how you
feel about your life?

Remember,

it is how your mind sees the world,

not

how the world sees your mind.

How do you feel

about what you see?

You
can only see
to the level
you are open to!
What is your
level of cultivated depth?

*When you
are no longer afraid to see,
you will.
Why would you not
want to see
what will free you?*

*If you believe
what you can't see,
are you seeing?
Are you open to learning
about
what you cannot see?*

*Do not believe
what you don't understand,
study
what you don't understand!
Is not study
how beliefs are replaced with knowing?*

Beliefs end
when seeing in the mind
becomes clear.
What do you trust,
beliefs
or
clear perception?

*Self-confidence, simply put,
is an understanding
of what you see.
Do you see confidently?*

Self-confidence,
in its purest form,
does not need to be explained.
When you know through experience,
do you need another to tell you
that you know?

*Y*our greatness is dependent

on what you see,

not

what others see.

Can another determine your greatness?

*The wonders
of the world await
when you open your mind
to see them.
What wonders do you see?*

*Do you care
if
your mind has clarity?*

Thinking is here ——————

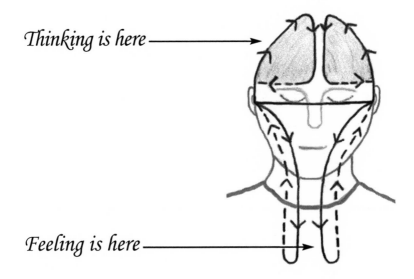

Feeling is here ——————

Standing on your own two feet
with a clear mind
is the only way
you can stand solidly.
How good is your mental stability?

If you are going to have clarity,

it has to be

from your thoughts,

not another's.

How clear

or

unclear are your thoughts?

*S*tep back

from the confusion of the world,

and

you will take a step closer

to the clarity of your own thoughts.

Are you

too caught up

in the outside world?

Simplicity

is

the way out of complexity.

How complex are your thoughts

and

do they need to be?

*The truth
is
an understanding
of clarity in your mind,
not another's.
Can another see the truth
for you?*

Clarity
does not come
from what others see,
it comes from what you see.
Is your mind clear?
If not, why?

*The only way to be clear

is

to not be affected

by that

which is unclear.

Are you clear about your thoughts?*

Watch carefully how you feel
about your thoughts
and
you will learn
about what bothers you and why.
What do you know
about what adversely affects you
and why?

Every negative reaction in your mind

is

a homework assignment

as to

why it is there.

Are you adversely affected by negativity,

and why?

It's good to be concerned,
but never worried.
Has worry ever helped you
to see clearly?
Is your worry a block to clarity?

*It is not wise
to convince yourself
right out of understanding.
Do you believe truth
or
perceive it?*

*The truth
seen by one
is the truth seen by all,
when
we all see clearly.
Does someone else decide how
you see life?*

The solutions to your problems
will appear
when you feel good about
accepting them.
Why would you not feel good
about accepting
what brings you clarity?

*Your purpose
can be
defined with a thought
when
you have a clear mind.
Is your purpose clear?*

Do you care
if
you have harmony in your life?

Thinking is here ⎯⎯⎯⎯⎯⎯⎯→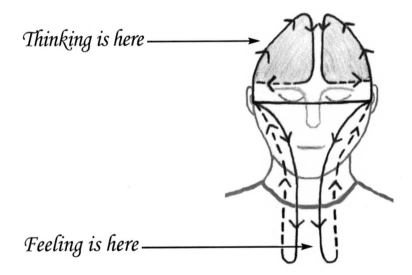

Feeling is here ⎯⎯⎯⎯⎯⎯⎯→

*The harmony
that gives you your freedom
is only determined
by your openness to experience it.
How open are you
to
harmony of mind?*

Open your mind
to that
which is fulfilling
by opening
to that which teaches you
about yourself.
Do you have healthy food for thought
in your life?

Care
for yourself
is what opens you up
to feel
what helps you.
Do you care how you feel
about yourself?

All physical and mental illness

is preceded

by tension on some level,

if you

look deep enough.

What do you know

about how deep your mental tension

is,

and how does it affect you?

Negativity is more prevalent
than harmony,
because it takes no awareness
to be ignorant.
How aware of your negativity are you
and
how does it affect you?

*A*nytime you give energy
to negative thoughts,
you
deplete your own energy.
Why do this?

*W*hen you
are drained mentally,
you
are weakened physically.
Why allow this to happen?
Who is in control
of
your mental state?

If you
are not paying attention
to your health,
who
is responsible for it?
Does your mind
have anything to do with your health?

*Negativity pulls you away
from yourself,
harmony brings you back!
Where do you
want to be?*

There is no bad

that comes

from true good.

Are your thoughts more harmonious

or

disharmonious?

*H*ealth
is a feeling of health,
and
at the deepest level
is found within
harmony of thought.
How often
do you feel mentally well?

*When your mind
lights up with a good thought,
your physical body
follows suit.
Are you in the dark
about
how you heal yourself?*

The whole key to feeling healthy

is to

feel good

about your health.

How do you feel

about your mental health?

The finest dining in the world

is

experienced

when an open and loving heart

is involved.

How well do you dine?

$\mathcal{Y}$ou
are not born to hurt,

you

are born to heal,

that's

the evolution of self-understanding.

You are either

in a process of hurting or healing.

Which way are you going?

*Harmonious thought

is

the way to heal!

Emotional pain can leave as quickly

as you can let it go.

Can you mentally let go

of that

which hurts you?

If not, why?*

To heal yourself,
you must let go of other people's suffering.
Taking on another's suffering
will not heal you.
Only harmony
can heal disharmony.
How do you
cultivate
harmony in your mind?

Relax the mind, heal the body;
this truth
is profoundly deep
when
you can feel it for yourself.
Do you know
how to relax your mind
and
how often do you do it?

*W*hen you
have calmed down
disharmony in the mind,
have you not
brought about a harmonious change?

How you
feel about yourself
when you go to sleep
is the difference
between a good night's sleep
or not.
How well do you sleep?
If not, why?

A good way to be

is

about everything

that makes life worth living.

Is not a calm mind each morning

a fine place to start your day?

How do you start your day,

calm or frantic?

The true understanding of harmony

is that

you

are worth more

than disharmony.

Why be disharmonious?

Chapter Twelve

Value

*Do you value
a heartfelt
way of being?*

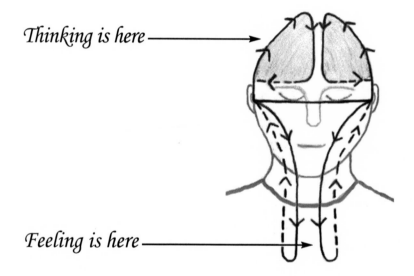

Thinking is here

Feeling is here

*Value all experience
that
enters your mind
and
you will learn from everything.
For what reason
would you
not value your life?*

The greatest value in life
that you hold
is your own.
How valuable are you?

*No one can value
your thoughts for you.
You are as rich or poor
as you feel.
How prosperous are you?*

*It is the simplest of gifts
that bring us
the deepest of life's riches.
What is a loving thought
worth to you?*

*Even a small thought
can touch you in a big way,
if
you are open.
Do you take the time to see
the nature of your thoughts?*

When you see your own beauty,

you

will open

to nature's beauty.

Where do you find beauty

in your life?

*The beauty of the world
does not open to us,
we open to it.
Are you open
to the beauty your mind
can perceive?*

*W*hen you're

not trying to experience beauty

is

when you experience it

at its deepest.

Can you help a sunset

be more beautiful?

*T*here's only one way

to add beauty to nature

and that is

to appreciate it.

Why would you not appreciate nature?

*W*hen you're
in appreciation of nature,
are you
not another one of its
beautiful wonders?

*We are all like flowers
in a garden.
To grow, each flower must accept
its own nature
to become
its full potential of beauty.
Are you open to growing
to your
full potential?*

We are all
a natural wonder
of ourselves,
when
we can learn to feel it.
How often do you have wonder
in your mind?

When you look into a still pond

you see a clear reflection.

Do you value

what you can learn

from self-reflection?

*The gift
you have always been
looking for
is
to find yourself.
Is not self-reflection
the way?*

Afterword

Now that you are done reading this book, you might ask, "Where do I go from here? How do I help myself to feel better?" These were the questions I asked myself when I was a teenager.

I did not set out to be a teacher. It is a long story, but it is just how my life unfolded. I also did not intend to be an author, but I have now written five books. If you feel that this book has inspired you and you want to learn more about yourself, you may wish to read some of my other work.

The Way is Within was finished in 1995 and was featured by Oprah Winfrey in a 2000 issue of *O, The Oprah Magazine*. When the magazine came out, I was in the midst of studying and researching the Kelee and did nothing to promote the book. There is a beautiful feeling that comes through the words in *The Way is Within*, and people would ask, "How did you attain that?" I would explain that it's because of a type of meditation that I practice. Then they would ask, "Well what kind of meditation do you practice?" At the time, I was practicing and teaching stillness of mind—a very specific form of stilling the mind which involved the Kelee. As the years unfolded, I became the founder of a form of meditation that evolved into what is now known as Kelee Meditation. In 1998 I wrote *The Silent Miracle* as a means of introducing Kelee Meditation to the world.

In *The Silent Miracle*, I use personal anecdotes to help people understand the underlying reasons for learning to quiet one's mind and then explain how to do Kelee Meditation.

In 2004 *The Kelee* was released and was a first-place winner at the San Diego Book Awards. By that time I had been teaching meditation for nearly twenty years and had gathered an enormous amount of information from simply observing the inner workings of the human mind. *The Kelee* offers a detailed explanation of the issues that people can hold onto and offers a way, through Kelee Meditation, to let go of negativity.

In December of 2005, a physician came to my office to learn Kelee Meditation (or what students fondly call "the Practice"). He took to the Practice like a duck to water. It is because of him that *The Basic Principles of the Kelee* was written. It offers a concise technical explanation of how to do Kelee Meditation.

My mentor used to say that everything in the universe moves from simple to complex and back to simple. After *The Basic Principles of the Kelee* was written, I realized that what I have come to understand about the Kelee is advanced and that in general our culture has difficulty encouraging the joy of learning. It is my wish that this book will inspire people to sit down for a few minutes every day and be still, so that their mind will naturally open to the beauty that life has to offer.

About the Author

When he was a young man, Ron W. Rathbun had a natural love for life and an innate curiosity in human behavior. Ron's education was unique. In his early twenties he met a man who had two PhDs and three master's degrees from California Technical Institute in Pasadena, California. He became Ron's teacher and mentor for twenty-eight years. Ron learned from his mentor that education is not only about learning from others, but to learn from one's own mind. Ron learned that unwarranted fear in the mind is what blocks one's learning process. In an effort to release his own fears, Ron studied the Kelee and consulted with his mentor until his passing in 2006.

Since the mid 1980s Ron W. Rathbun has studied and researched how negativity adversely affects the mind and body. His work is presently in a medical study at a university in California to measure how releasing fear can decrease anxiety, depression, and stress. He currently teaches physicians, health care professionals, and people from all walks of life how to understand the inner workings of the mind and their relationship with the Kelee.

Contact Us

What each person brings to the world is what they have within. It is our mission to offer, to all those who are seeking, a way to internally heal one's own mind through Kelee Meditation. For it is the condition of one's Kelee that influences one's emotional and physical health and wellness.

The Kelee Foundation is a 501(c)(3) nonprofit, tax-exempt organization. It is generously funded by the donations of its dedicated students and all those who recognize the health benefits of a clear mind. Please feel free to contact us if you are interested in learning more.

Web site: www.thekelee.org

Mailing
address: Kelee Foundation
P.O. Box 373
Oceanside, CA 92049-0373

Breinigsville, PA USA
22 September 2009
224539BV00001B/4/P